PLYM PUBS
PAST & PRESENT

The 'Harvest Home'
and a hundred others

written and compiled by

CHRIS ROBINSON

edited by Terry Guswell

additional research Doreen Mole

PEN&INK PUBLISHING

British Library Cataloguing-in-Publication Data
Robinson, Chris, 1954-
    Pubs of Plymouth past and present: the Harvest Home and a hundred others
    1. Bars (Drinking establishments) - England - Plymouth - History
    2. Bars (Drinking establishments) - England - Plymouth - Pictorial works
    I. Title
    647.9'5'0942358

    ISBN 0951074733

Design: Chris Robinson, Terry Guswell, Rob Warren and Clive Hooper
Copyright © Chris Robinson 1996

First Published November 1996

Published by
Pen & Ink Publishing
34 New Street
Barbican
Plymouth PL1 2NA, Devon
01752-228120

Printed and bound in Great Britain
by Latimer Trend & Company Ltd
Estover Close
Plymouth PL6 7PL, Devon

PLYMOUTH PUBS PAST & PRESENT

Harvest Home - Tavistock Road - *Demolished 1964* .... ❑
Abbey - St. Andrew Street - *Now Kitty O'Hanlons* .... ❑
Admiral MacBride - The Barbican .... ❑
Albemarle - Whitleigh Green .... ❑
Albert - Charlotte Street, Devonport .... ❑
Albion Inn - Pembroke Street, Devonport - *Demolished 1955* .... ❑
Artillery Arms - Admiralty Street, Stonehouse .... ❑
Avondale - Keyham Road .... ❑
Barley Sheaf - Catherine Street, Devonport - *Closed 1945* .... ❑
Barley Sheaf - Cambridge Street - *Closed 1957* .... ❑
Barnstaple Inn - Princess Street - *Demolished 1958* .... ❑
Bedford Vaults - Old Town Street - *Demolished 1965* .... ❑
Black Prince - Laira Place, Prince Rock .... ❑
Blue Bird - Eggbuckland Road, Higher Compton .... ❑
Blue Peter - Pomphlett Road, Plymstock .... ❑
Breton Arms - Buckwell Street - *Now O'Neills* .... ❑
Bristol Castle - Duncan Street .... ❑
Bull and Bush - Uxbridge Drive, Ernesettle .... ❑
Burton Boys - Exeter Street - *Demolished 1981* .... ❑
Camels Head - Wolseley Road - *Demolished 1988* .... ❑
Castle - Union Street .... ❑
Charlotte St. Ale & Porter House - Charlotte St. - *Demolished 1958* .... ❑
Cherry Tree - Ham Drive .... ❑
Clifton - Clifton Street .... ❑
Crabtree Inn - London Road - *Demolished 1971* .... ❑
Dartmoor Inn - Tavistock Road - *Demolished c.1900* .... ❑
Devon Inn - Buckwell Street - *Closed 1954* .... ❑
Druids Arms - Russell Street - *Demolished 1954* .... ❑
Duke of Cornwall - High Street, Stonehouse - *Demolished c.1955* .... ❑
Duke Street Inn - Duke Street, Devonport - *Demolished 1958* .... ❑
Empire - Cambridge Street - *Demolished c.1958* .... ❑
Falcon - Melville Road, Ford .... ❑

Oporto - York Street - *Demolished early 1960s* .... ❑

Picken's Wine Vaults - Whimple Street - *Closed 1954* .... ❑

Portland Inn - James Street, North Road East - *Closed 1956* .... ❑

Post Office Inn - Market Street, Devonport - *Demolished c.1956* .... ❑

Prince Alfred - Clarence Place, Stonehouse .... ❑

Prince of Wales - Keyham Road - *Closed 1992* .... ❑

Prospect Inn - Prospect Place - *Closed 1952* .... ❑

Red Lion - Cambridge Street - *Demolished 1961* .... ❑

Revenue - Duke Street/Tavistock Road - *Demolished c.1964* .... ❑

Rose and Crown - Pembroke Street - *Demolished c.1960* .... ❑

Royal Naval Arms - Saltash Road, Keyham .... ❑

Salutation - Stillman Street, Barbican - *Demolished 1897* .... ❑

Ship Inn - Millbay Road - *Demolished 1960* .... ❑

Sir Francis Drake - Camden Street - *Closed 1973* .... ❑

Somerset Arms - North Road West .... ❑

Spread Eagle - Treville Street - *Closed 1957* .... ❑

Sugar Refinery - Duke Street/Saltash Street - *Demolished c.1964* .... ❑

Tandem - Octagon Street - *Demolished early 1960s* .... ❑

Tap and Barrel - Ashford Crescent, Mannamead .... ❑

Terminus - Paradise Place, Stoke .... ❑

Three Crowns - The Parade, Barbican .... ❑

Three Ferrets - Charlotte Street .... ❑

Tiger - Dorchester Avenue .... ❑

Trafalgar Inn - Ebrington Street .... ❑

Trelawny Hotel - Wolseley Road, St. Budeaux .... ❑

Turks Head - St. Andrew's Street - *Demolished 1860* .... ❑

Unity - Eastlake Street .... ❑

Unity - Park Street/Garden Street - *Demolished c.1904* .... ❑

Victory - Farm Lane .... ❑

Welcome Inn - Richmond Street - *Closed 1954* .... ❑

Wellington - Wellington Street .... ❑

Which You Please - Keyham Road/St. Levan Road - *Closed c.1973* .... ❑

Woodside - Gasking Street - *Now Fool & Firkin* .... ❑

Wyndham Arms - Stoke Road .... ❑

ACKNOWLEDGEMENTS

Thanks to Alan Cooper, editor of the *Evening Herald*, and to Stuart Fraser, Pete Hale and Chris Collins, of the features desk, who for many years have been knocking my weekly pieces into shape for the Saturday local history page in the *Herald* - where these articles first appeared. Thanks to Doreen Mole and Terry Guswell of the Old Plymouth Society, without whom you probably would not be holding a copy of this book. Their editing and enthusiasm, Doreen's additional research and Terry's hours of inputting, adjusting and formatting all helped bring the first volume of this series to fruition earlier than I could have otherwise have hoped for.

To Rob Warren for his research and general management of our New Street premises. To my partner in all this, Clare Robinson, who has visited with me almost all of those pubs still standing in Plymouth today - in the line of duty of course. And to Chris Savery, old friend and fellow researcher in the early stages of this project.

My thanks are also due to Ann Landers, John Smith and Margaret Willcocks of the Local Studies Department of the Central Library, and to John Elliott, area librarian west, and county librarian, Alison Shute, for the use of library material. To Mark Tosdevin for allowing us to go through and use material from the archives of Plymouth City Museum. Similarly to Alan Cooper, once more, for allowing us to use material from the *Western Morning News* and *Evening Herald* Library. To Graham Watson, David Ashby and Lyn Miller at the Plymouth Magistrates Court for their courtesy and invaluable assistance. To Henry Horwill who donated to the Local Studies Department his two very thorough manuscript volumes on the licensees of all known pubs of Devonport Past and Present (up to 1975) and to Mr. Broderick who over many years compiled perhaps the most remarkable set of records on Devonport ever produced. Thanks too to the many people who have sent in or loaned me photographs of old Pubs of Plymouth, in particular Coleen Fry, Miss Moss, Mrs. B. Tozer, and Eileen Bateman. Incidentally I am always on the lookout and should you know of the whereabouts of any old pictures of Plymouth Pubs ... please get in touch.

And finally thanks to father, Des Robinson, who has stood me many a pint in many of the hostelries here featured. Cheers ... everyone!

Plymouth
October 1996

INTRODUCTION

All the articles you will see in this book first appeared on the regular Saturday local history page that I produce for the *Evening Herald*. It is the aim of the series to try and cover all of the "Pubs of Plymouth - Past and Present". Currently there are something like two hundred and twenty licensed premises in Plymouth classed as pubs and there are certainly a great deal more than two hundred and twenty that once existed in the Three Towns and are no longer with us today. The book you have in your hands now is intended to be the first of several volumes binding the series together in batches of a hundred. In an ideal world it would indeed be nice to try and cover all of the pubs, the problem however is always going to be finding a photograph or illustration of some of those inns, taverns and beerhouses that are no more - some of which were perhaps only open for a few years or so. If you know of the whereabouts of any pictorial Plymouth Pub material ... please let us know.

Pubs are special places for a great number of reasons, even for those who may seldom, or never, venture inside them they are an integral part of our visual and cultural environment. People use them in giving directions ... "you turn right just past the George" ... They are used as meeting places - where better or more convenient to arrange to meet someone if there is a possibility one or other party might be late. There are all too few places where you can sit and wait in the warm without feeling too conspicuous.

Public houses are exactly that - public houses, houses where the public can go and sit or stand, take refuge or whatever. In an era when churches are increasingly being left locked for much of the time, the number of venues that fit this bill is becoming increasingly small - it's hard to sit in a restaurant for too long without eating, but it is possible to make a drink last an awfully long time if you want it to. But this is not really supposed to be a document promoting pubs, rather it is simply an historical review of one hundred and one Plymouth Pubs, where over the years doubtless millions have whiled away many, many hours. To that extent it is almost a celebration of local hostelries along with many

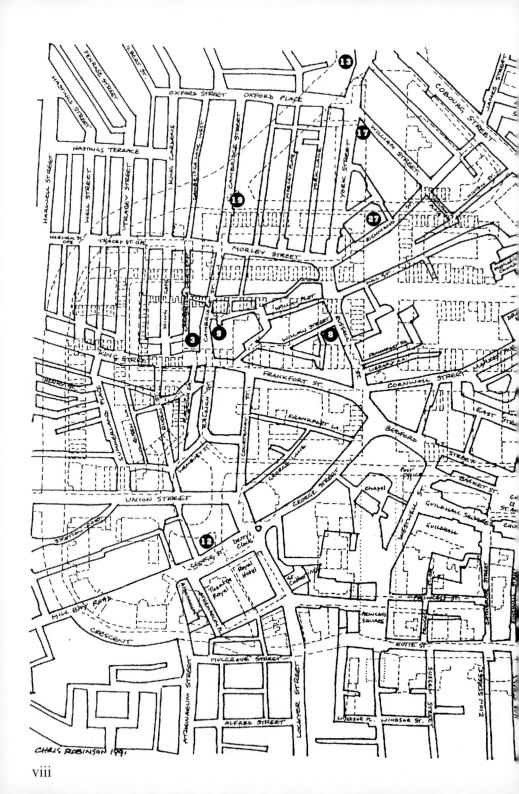

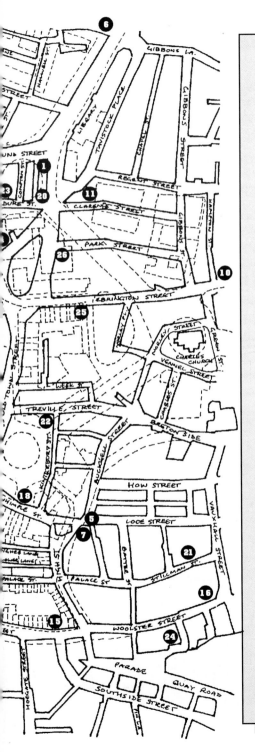

This list extends *only* to those City Centre pubs featured in this volume. There were - and indeed still are - many others.

The dotted lines show the City Centre as it is today.

names of those who have served as licensees in the last two hundred years.

Over 1600 names are indexed at the back of the book and no doubt there are many omissions and there could have been many more. For the years prior to 1920 we have relied primarily on the information supplied in the collection of Street Directories available in the Local Studies Department of Plymouth Central Library. There they have a substantial, but by no means complete, set of directories from the 1840s onwards (there are a handful of earlier volumes) and so the information pulled from them does not entirely give us as full a picture as we could wish for - but it is an excellent starting point for anyone wishing to take their research on any pub further.

From 1921 onwards the information in this book has been taken directly from the records of the Licensing Magistrates and therefore it is about as accurate as one could wish for. It should be remembered though that it is a list of licensees, not necessarily managers, or head-barmen or barmaids, and generally we have given formal forenames, not nicknames or other names by which the landlord or landlady might have been known. There is no hidden agenda in the selection of pubs you find here, they are taken from all parts of the modern city, and as stated earlier, it is the intention to cover all, or as many as we can find pictures for, of the Pubs of Plymouth Past and Present in subsequent volumes. As perhaps the most famous of all of the Plymouth Pubs Past we have chosen to open our account with the pub on the cover - the Harvest Home. The prominent location of this fine old building made it a much loved landmark and one which served as a reminder of the old pre-war city centre longer than almost all the other Blitz survivors. However that alone would not account for some of the splendid pre-war photographs we found of the building, including the splendid interior shot on the back cover, from Christmas 1932, and the glorious, heavily populated, view here, taken sometime around 1918.

If you ever supped ale in the Harvest Home I hope these pictures bring back happy memories, as indeed I hope of all the pictures of the pubs here featured in this first volume of Plymouth Pubs Past and Present. Here's to it leaving you thirsty for more!

HARVEST HOME

This well-remembered and well-loved corner pub at the junction of Tavistock Road and Pound Street was pulled down on Sunday 29 November 1964. Its site today is somewhere around the top of the circular pedestrian centre in the middle of the Drake's Circus roundabout. It was built as a coaching house in the first half of the nineteenth century when this stretch of 'Old Town without' became Tavistock Street (Tavistock Road from the late 1860s). Pound Street, incidentally (at the end of Cobourg Street) was so named because of the old animal pound there.

The distinctive archway to the stable yard and the old ostler's bell were ever features of this prominently placed public house. Chubb, Pearse and Hamley were among the early long-serving landlords here in the pre-motor car days.

For many years an Octagon Brewery pub - the old octagonal logo can still be seen here - it became a Simonds house shortly before it closed.

PLYMOUTH PUBS PAST & PRESENT

1

THE ABBEY

Standing on the oldest known inn site in Plymouth, the Abbey was built in St. Andrew Street, following the demolition of the mediaeval Turk's Head in 1861. St. Andrew's Street itself is one of the oldest thoroughfares in the city, although since 1979 its line has been interrupted by Plymouth Magistrates' Court. Until the 1930s an ancient terrace of buildings known as Abbey Place ran from the corner of St. Andrew Street, opposite this pub, across to the top of Finewell Street and the Prysten House. Curiously enough it is this building - the Prysten House - which indirectly gave its name both to Abbey Place and the Abbey Hotel. Long thought, albeit mistakenly, to have been a place with ecclesiastical connections, the house, built by Thomas Yogge in the fifteenth century, was being referred to as the Old Abbey at least 250 years ago. The picture of an old Abbey ruins on the inn sign is no more than an attractive piece of fiction. Currently known as Kitty O'Hanlons (since 1994) this was the first 'Irish' pub in Plymouth. Although this is the current landlady's first pub she could be said to have the trade in her blood - her parents met in the erstwhile Camel's Head when her grandparents were the licensees there.

PLYMOUTH
P BS
PAST & PRESENT

2

ADMIRAL MACBRIDE

Patrick Shea was licensee here in 1798, at that time Admiral John MacBride was still alive but no longer living in Plymouth where he had been based for many years.

Although he grew up in Ireland, John MacBride was born in Scotland. He joined the Royal Navy in 1754 after some years as a Merchant Seaman. His Plymouth residence was Leigham House on the site of the modern estate.

MacBride sat as an MP for Plymouth, from 1784-1790, and it was he who was largely responsible for the passing of the Parliamentary Bill which approved the construction of the pier that runs east from the front of the pub and which together with the old east pier made Sutton Harbour into a much safer haven than it had previously been.

It is thought that the pub itself was built at the same time and stands on reclaimed land. The original "Mayflower Steps" were probably located somewhere towards the back of the pub.

PLYMOUTH
P**U**BS
PAST & PRESENT

THE ALBEMARLE

LICENSEES

1960 **David Walters**
1967 **Alexander Kelman**
1967 **Russell Know**
1968 **Thomas Marshall**
1973 **Henry Gilmour**
1974 **Robert Bittles**
1976 **David Begley**
1981 **William Hannigan**
1984 **David Earl**
1990 **Joseph Killman**
1992 **John Green**
1993 **Richard Fullock**
1993 **Charlotte Jeffery**
1994 **Ricky Clark & Caroline Luxton**
1994 **Ian Martin**
1995 **Eleanor Ewart & Ian Martin**
1996 **Vanessa Kelly**
1996 **Roy Wakeling**

Until Whitleigh was developed after the Second World War the basic layout of the manor had altered little since the Domesday Survey with its manor house and two farms. It would doubtless have been almost recognisable to Robert d'Albermarla who became its new Norman lord after the Conquest over nine hundred years ago.

The pub, which is built approximately on the site of one of the old farm buildings, is named after this major local landowner. However Albermarle doesn't appear to have lived here, rather he established a family base for himself in Stoke - hence Stoches D'Abermala or Stoke Damerel where his family remained until the 1300s. Whitleigh itself he let to a tenant - Osulf.

There is incidentally a story that d'Albamarla was named after his shield which bore an image of a white blackbird - an albino merle, although the more favoured suggestion is that his name came from Aumale in eastern Normandy where his family had its roots.

PLYMOUTH
P**U**BS
PAST & PRESENT

THE ALBERT

It stands on the site of the Charlotte Street Ale and Porter House and Ophelia Evans became its first official licensee in September 1958. She and Sydney Evans then saw this new pub through its first eighteen years. Originally known as the Albert Gate after the nearby gate of the mid-nineteenth century Keyham Steam Yard, the pub is now known more simply as the Albert.

The Gate itself, which was closed in 1966, was so named because it stood at the bottom of Albert Road (the former Navy Row).

This in turn took its name from Prince Albert (1819-61), Queen Victoria's consort, who was alive when the Keyham Yard was opened and whose portrait now adorns the inn sign for this modern Plymouth pub.

PLYMOUTH
P▮BS
PAST & PRESENT

5

ALBION INN

At one time there were ten or more hotels and inns in Pembroke Street, one of them was the Albion. It stood towards the western end of the street on the north corner of Pembroke Street and Canterbury Street - where new flats are already replacing those that were built here sometime after this photograph was taken in the mid-1950s.

Albion is an old, somewhat poetic, name for England, probably arising out of the Latin "albus" meaning white, a reference to the white cliffs along stretches of the southern coast. Many naval ships have borne that name and before the local rugby club of that name came into being there were a number of Albion inns and hotels in the Three Towns, now there are none.

The first reference to this as the Albion came in 1877, earlier records suggest that it may once have been known as the King William.

PLYMOUTH
P*BS
PAST & PRESENT

ARTILLERY ARMS

It is likely that the Artillery Arms in Stonehouse is the only pub in Plymouth to have had at least ten different women serving as licensees in the last hundred years. Eliza Partridge, who appears to have succeeded her husband (here since 1905 at least) sometime during the First World War, has probably been the longest serving lady here. Eliza was here until 1939 and since her time no man has held this licence on his own for more than four years (and that was Robert Porter just after the Second World War).

Situated as it is right next to the Royal Marine Barracks, the Artillery has doubtless seen more servicemen pass through its doors than most Plymouth pubs, and war and artillery talk has doubtless loomed large in the conversations here over the years, this century and last. Nevertheless it's hard to imagine that when first opened, this Admiralty Street pub would have been right on the water's edge and that among the first men to use this beerhouse (as it was until 1958) would have been those who were taken from the Barracks, by boat, across to Staddon Heights to use the famous brick wall firing range there. However before either the pub or the wall were very old, the wall was declared unsafe, because of the advances in artillery (notably the new Lee-Metford rifles) around 1890. Both wall and pub however still stand firm today.

PLYMOUTH
PUBS
PAST & PRESENT

7

THE AVONDALE

Said to be named in honour of a Scottish Duke who had men working in the yard at some time, the "Avondale Arms" was originally known as the "Sportsman Arms" and appears to be contemporary with Keyham Yard, the gates of which it stands opposite.

Thomas Hewlett is recorded as, probably, its first licensee in 1850 and in almost 150 years of trading from No.1 Keyham Road, the Avondale would appear to be remarkable in having had less than ten licensees in all that time, and just four in the last 100 and more years. Chiefly responsible for that remarkable statistic is Arthur Squire who has been landlord here since 1950 (the year Starkey Knight and Ford purchased the pub) and is almost certainly the longest serving licensee, in one pub, in Plymouth today.

PLYMOUTH
P**U**BS
PAST & PRESENT

BARLEY SHEAF

It stood near the entrance to Devonport market, at the end of Catherine Street at the junction with Market Street and Duke Street. Closed since the war, it nevertheless was still standing many years later. In 1954 its licence was removed to the Grapes Tavern in Charlotte Street and soon afterwards this part of Devonport found itself inside the new wall around the extended dockyard.

The name is one of the oldest in the pub canon and is a variant on the old Barley Mow; barley being one of the main ingredients of beer. The simplest way to advertise that ale was on sale was to hang up a sign showing a stack, mow or sheaf of the bearded cereal. One of Devonport's oldest pubs, our earliest reference to it shows that Elizabeth Hancock was licensee here during the Napoleonic Wars (from at least 1798 to 1814) - a boom time for the town.

PLYMOUTH
P**BS
PAST & PRESENT

BARLEY SHEAF

If you imagine driving down the middle of Raleigh Street, from the bottom of Royal Parade and going right through the shops directly in front of you, on the northern side of New George Street, there at the back entrance, you would find the site of the Barley Sheaf, on the corner of what was once King Street and Cambridge Street.

John Laskey was the licensee here in 1847, when it was the Barley Mow and the address was given as Frankfort Street. In 1881, it was now, without moving, in King Street. It appears to have become known as the Old Barley Sheaf in the 1890s and on its closure in late 1957 the licence was transferred to the pub newly-built at the junction of New George Street and Market Avenue - originally known as the Barley Sheaf, then as Trader Jacks, it is the Corner House today.

PLYMOUTH
P█BS
PAST & PRESENT

BARNSTAPLE INN

It stood in what became known as Princes Street but which was for most of the nineteenth century known as Princess Street - an altogether more logical name given the proximity of King Street and Queen Street. Today most of this thoroughfare is known as Granby Way although just behind the Forum a small part survives as Princes Street. Most of it has gone however, including the Barnstaple Inn as shown here.

Located on the northern side of the street, east of the junction with Marlborough Street, one of the earliest recorded licensees here was Richard Mackay who appears to have been here for the best part of twenty years at least, between 1812 and 1830. John Warren was then listed as licensee for the next twenty years, before we find Richard Mackay back behind the bar - the same one or a son perhaps? Towards the end of the nineteenth century Baker is another name that crops up twice after an interval, while the longest serving licensee here this century, before the pub's demolition in the late 1950s, was Ethel Philips, who came here as Ethel Williams in 1929.

PLYMOUTH
P**U**BS
PAST & PRESENT

11

BEDFORD VAULTS

On the western side of C&A - inside the shop - a little way back from the main Eastlake Street entrance, is the spot on which the Bedford Vaults (formerly the Bedford Inn) once stood.

In the fine view below from the 1890s, with an advertisement for Turner's grocery in neighbouring Drake Street, the Bedford Vaults stood on the corner of a small opening, possibly called Caxton Mews, off Old Town Street which eventually led to the stables.

In private hands for many years, it was later acquired by Starkey, Knight & Ford. Whitbread then closed it in July 1965. It was demolished soon after to make way for what looks like being the comparatively short-lived Drake's Circus complex.

PLYMOUTH
P BS
PAST & PRESENT

BLACK PRINCE

It opened as the Laira Hotel in 1868 and at that time the view from the back of the building would have been extensive. No streets behind just green fields, even the railway was still a few years away. Thomas Rowe was the licensee here for the best part of those early years, throughout the 1870s and into the 1890s when he was succeeded by, in all probability, his son William. For over a hundred years it remained as the Laira Hotel and then in March 1981 it was renamed the Black Prince. The prince in question being Edward, Prince of Wales and son of Edward III. A skilled soldier famed for his black armour, the prince visited Plymouth on many occasions and he is recorded as having made a grant to some "poor brothers" who may well have been the nearby friars at Friary.

In 1358 the Prince ordered a warship to be built in Plymouth and although it is the first we have written evidence of it was doubtless not the first to be built here.

PLYMOUTH PUBS PAST & PRESENT

BLUE BIRD

A former tea house on Eggbuckland Road, Higher Compton, the Blue Bird acquired its licence in 1944 following the surrender of the licence of the former Washington Hotel. The Washington was one of many Plymouth pubs to be lost during the war, it stood in the erstwhile Washington Place off Millbay Road, Albert Thomas had been there over sixteen years when war was declared. The Blue Bird meanwhile was re-launched as a pub in 1944 with William Redman as its landlord. At that time there was very little development between the pub and what is now the Parkway. A large part of the trade for the tea house came from the visitors to the cemetery.

The current sign for the pub incidentally features a picture of the streamlined car the "Bluebird" that Sir Malcolm Campbell broke the 300 mph land speed record in 1935.

PLYMOUTH PUBS PAST & PRESENT

BLUE PETER

By no means the only pub of this name in Britain, the Blue Peter in Pomphlett Road was thought to take its name from the naval flag traditionally hoisted twenty-four hours before a ship leaves port. Blue with a central white square, the flag appears in the background of the current inn sign of this Plymstock pub.

Interestingly enough though this and one or two later Blue Peter pubs owes its name to the Derby winner of 1939. The first inn sign to hang here showed a representation of the head of Lord Roseberry's winner ... And who knows, one day the BBC children's television programme, first aired in October 1958, may one day be commemorated in the naming of a pub.

PLYMOUTH PUBS PAST & PRESENT

15

BRETON ARMS

The Breton Arms - a post-war pub with a name that carries a nudging reference back to events that rocked the local community over five hundred years ago. Like Breton or Briton-side itself, this commemorates the series of Breton raids on the town, notably in 1377, 1400 and 1403, the last of which was particularly devastating and saw a great part of the eastern side of the town burnt and destroyed. It was however to be the last time that such widespread destruction was visited upon the town - until that was, the Blitz of the Second World War.

Strangely enough though without that more recent devastation the Breton Arms would almost certainly have never have been built for it stands on the very fringe of the massive redevelopment of the city centre, where it somewhat unfortunately sits right across the original entrance to Looe Street. It is a great pity that the street topography from Looe Street to Whimple Street, where it was intersected by what was High Street, ever had to be restructured for here was the old market cross and the very heart of old Plymouth. But time never stands still and since 1960 this typical period piece has seen various internal changes and in 1996 it was restyled O'Neills.

PLYMOUTH
P U B S
PAST & PRESENT

BRISTOL CASTLE

Its address today is No. 6 Duncan Street, but the old St. John Street sign is still there, a little rusty, but that's all. Otherwise these two-buildings-in-one that have long since been the Bristol Castle are little changed, outwardly at least, from the mid-fifties shot of them we see here. The thick-walled slate-hung part is clearly the oldest element of the pub and apparently dates back to 1645 (originally two cottages with stables and hayloft above, it is said that this was an old coaching inn on the way to the ferry). The pub is now easily the oldest structure in the immediate area. The original neighbouring houses, the lamp-post, the old cobbles are all long gone, swept away years ago when this part of Devonport was redeveloped. Happily though the pub not only continues to thrive today but it has also retained its name, although it is not the original name of the hostelry; that appears to have been the Joiner's Arms, a name lost in the late 1860s.

Quite what the reason for the change was we do not know. There is a picture of the old steam engine that went by the name of the Bristol Castle in one bar and in the other there are drawings and plans of the old Bristol Castle itself. Built soon after the Norman Conquest, the castle was demolished at the instruction of Cromwell and in the 1660s the site was developed for civilian housing. There is a suggestion that part of the old castle stonework was shipped here and used in the construction of this building - hence the name.

PLYMOUTH
P⬛BS
PAST & PRESENT

17

BULL AND BUSH

When this pub was being built on the new Ernesettle estate in 1957/58 it was felt that it would be a good idea if the modern building was to be given a traditional name and one of the most common and ancient inn names in this country is The Bull.

There would appear to be three principal popular explanations for this; a certain religious significance, from bulla, an ecclesiastical seal; the once common, and, in places, compulsory, practice of bull-baiting and thirdly the creature's significance in animal husbandry. There are many basic bull name variations, one of the most famous being the old Bull and Bush (the bush or the vine being one of the earliest signs of all for a drinking establishment).

Here in Ernesettle none of the historical connotations above apply but the idea of this particular name for a pub so close to the local Bush Radio Factory (now Toshiba) where so many of the new Ernesettle settlers were employed, was too good to pass on.

PLYMOUTH PUBS PAST & PRESENT

BURTON BOYS

It stood in Exeter Street just along from its junction with Sutton Road and was pulled down for the sake of just a few feet projecting into the line of the redeveloped highway in 1981. A sad loss for a pub that appears to have already survived one major upheaval when it was rebuilt just before the Second World War. Previously it was just an ale house and James Mitchell its proprietor brewed white ale here. The pub's name, incidentally came from a corruption of the 'Breton Boys' in acknowledgement of the annual commemorative Freedom Fighting that used to take place in a field near here between the Old Town Boys and the Breton Boys. The fighting, which celebrated the thwarting of the Breton Raids, notably that of 1403, was in later years relocated to the area we now know as Freedom Fields. The Burton Boys itself appears to have the unusual distinction of having had only two families of licensees in its last 100 years .... the last two being father and son - Gardner and Maurice Hogg. Today the Hogg pub link continues with Maurice's daughter Maureen, whose husband Keith Ashford is the joint licensee with Sue Constantine of the Maritime in Southside Street.

PLYMOUTH
P BS
PAST & PRESENT

CAMEL'S HEAD

Built in 1825, seemingly thanks to the Reverend C.T. Trelawny-Ross for the benefit of the men laying down the new road from Plymouth, it was pulled down in 1988 when that same road was widened.

Known for all but ten years as the Camel's Head it was renamed the Submarine in 1978, in recognition of all the submarine work and activity that occurs on the built-up mouth of Camel's Head Creek. Ernest Holderness, the longest serving post-war licensee was landlord at that time and the name change was prompted by a change of ownership as the pub was bought that year by Bass from Courage. It stood opposite Ferndale Road and next to an old cinema.

PLYMOUTH
P⬛BS
PAST & PRESENT

THE CASTLE

John Yeo, a name more commonly associated with one of Plymouth's older department stores, was the name of the first licensee we have record of at the Castle. John was here by 1864 when the premises were advertised as "The Castle Wine and Spirit Vaults and Bowling Alley". One of at least three Yeos who have been here over the years, the last would appear to have been H.F. Yeo at the beginning of this century. But there was by no means a consistent succession of Yeos, as Robert Eden was here for most of the 1880s and throughout the 1890s.

While the Castle is a common enough pub name across the country, most take their name from a neighbouring fortification rather than, as appears to be the case in this instance, the fact that the pub has been blessed with a few fort-like features. Speculation suggests that a number of "rogue" Castles have their origin in the saying "An Englishman's home is his castle", perhaps it applies here too.

PLYMOUTH PUBS PAST & PRESENT

21

CHARLOTTE STREET ALE & PORTER HOUSE

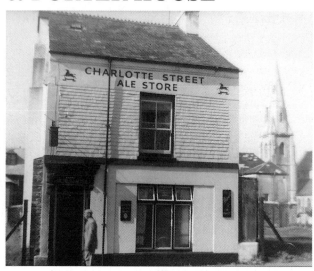

Number 32 Charlotte Street was built soon after the beginning of the nineteenth century along with the rest of the street it stood in. A small but famous Ale and Porter House it officially took its name from the street itself - which was named after Princess Charlotte Augusta, daughter of the Prince of Wales, the future George IV - however it was long known more popularly as Smokey or Smoky Joe's.

Run by the Sloggett family from at least 1838 through to 1914, Henry and Rosina Bond where here for a number of years after the Second World War, while Dora Jones had it for the last five years of its life. It was demolished in 1958 and The Albert now stands in its place.

THE CHERRY TREE

Pubs that stand outside of the main area covered by the Three Towns of Plymouth, Stonehouse or Devonport in the late 1890s tend either to be small (although sometimes expanded), centuries old village pubs or large twentieth century, "modern", estate pubs. The Cherry Tree, off Ham Drive, is undoubtedly one of the latter. Added to the Plymouth lists on the 1st April 1937 the pub was built close to the late lamented Pennycross Stadium, an exciting arena that witnessed all manner of sporting activities from Greyhound Racing through Speedway to Stock Car Racing.

One of the early licensees of the pub however was more used to appearing in another local stadium - Home Park. This was the ex-Argyle player (as opposed to England cricketer) Fred Titmuss. In more recent times the longest serving licensee here has been Harry (Nick) Nicholls - a man who grew up with beer in his blood. He was brought up in the Passage House Inn at Cattedown which his parents, Flo and Harry kept for over 20 years.

PLYMOUTH
P■BS
PAST & PRESENT

THE CLIFTON

In the 1860s Clifton Place was laid out running almost at right-angles to North Hill. Providence Street, running parallel to North Hill, appeared soon afterwards and then, in line with that and reaching up to Clifton Place, Clifton Street was formed. A few doors down from the top of the street was and still is the Clifton.

Licensee here from 1873 through to the mid-1890s was John Bickle and then after a couple of changes the pub settled down to more than twenty years of proprietorship by the Chilcotts, Levi then Ellen, who had the pub through the First World War until 1920. A few more changes then the Farmers, Stanley then Marion (Davies from 1955), took the Clifton from 1940 through to 1959.

Reputedly Plymouth's luckiest pub, three regulars have won more than a million pounds each in two seperate wins on the National Lottery in the mid-1990s.

PLYMOUTH
P**BS
PAST & PRESENT

CRABTREE INN

It stood on the old London Road, opposite the Lee Moor tramway, and just beyond the point where Military Road branches off towards Laira Battery and Efford Fort. In 1971 it was pulled down, as were the adjacent cottages, so that the road could be widened to accommodate the new dual carriageway. A sad end for what was thought to have been one of Plymouth's oldest public houses. Before the building of Longbridge this would have been a popular resort for travellers crossing the Plym at what was the lowest crossing point, the Ebb Ford (hence Efford), below the medieval Plym Bridge itself.

William Litton, who came here in 1962 was the pub's last licensee.

PLYMOUTH
PUBS
PAST & PRESENT

DARTMOOR INN

It stood in what is now the small car park just below Sherwell Church, in Tavistock Road, but it was standing long before the Church was built. In the 1850s when John Orchard was landlord (he also had the Wine and Spirit Vaults in York Street) it was just a beerhouse, known then as the Dartmoor Inn. During Joseph Carah's time here it became the Dartmoor Hotel and as can be seen from this, and another photograph, taken around the same time, during the late 1890s this curious little, partly slate-hung, building became known as Cole's Dartmoor Hotel. In 1897 however to celebrate the centenary of the Norley Chapel (out of which Sherwell itself had indirectly grown) a fund was amassed to purchase the Inn and the lessee, Mrs Barnicott was later paid £585 to give vacant possession and thereby surrender the remaining nine years of her lease. It was demolished soon afterwards.

PLYMOUTH PUBS PAST & PRESENT

DEVON INN

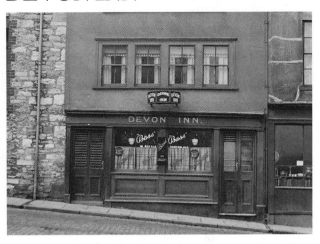

The original, pre-war Buckwell Street ran from what is now the middle of Bretonside Bus Station and was then Treville Street, through to the top of Looe Street, where it ended. Today it runs from the south-western corner of the bus station, a little way out from the top of How Street and Looe Street, and includes most of what used to be High Street, running down to meet Notte Street. The Breton Arms is the only pub in that stretch today but in old Buckwell Street there were a number of beerhouses over the years; the Nag's Head, the Masonic, the Crown and Sceptre and here at No.3 Buckwell Street - the Devon Inn. Just a few doors down from the Looe Street junction, the Devon was clearly quite an ancient building but its early history is rather vague and little is known apart from the names of a few nineteenth century licensees - Turner, Allen and Roberts among them.

Licensee Frederick Martin had been here fifteen years when war broke out in 1939 and he was succeeded in 1941 by Arthur Howard. Interestingly enough the licence here was not finally surrendered until 1954 when Israel Bertie Black had it removed to the Octagon Restaurant.

PLYMOUTH PUBS PAST & PRESENT

DRUIDS ARMS

It stood in Russell Street, on the corner of Willow Street, on a site that is now to be found in the car park that is bounded by the rear of the shops in New George Street, Armada Way, Cornwall Street and Woolworth's. An early Victorian beerhouse it enjoyed a little over 100 years of trading before finally becoming a victim of the post-war redevelopment of the city centre in 1954. Harold Lee was the landlord here when war was declared and for many years he brewed his own beer here. The name is a common enough one, in many places it is a reference to the ancient Celtic priesthood of Britain and Gaul (a religious order that venerated oak and mistletoe and believed in immortality and reincarnation), elsewhere it can be an indication that this was where the United Ancient Order of Druids used to meet (this was a friendly society founded in 1781), the term is also still in use to describe Celtic Bards and officers of the Welsh National Eisteddfod.

PLYMOUTH
P▪BS
PAST & PRESENT

DUKE OF CORNWALL

After the war it stood in isolation for some years but 100 years ago it was but one of 10 licensed premises in the old High Street, Stonehouse.

The character and appearance of the western end of High Street has changed greatly since then, and since the war, and since the closure of the hospital. Today only the re-named Royal Naval Hospital Inn is there outside the former hospital walls as a reminder of what used to be.

The near door here was the entrance to the pub and the bar counter was just behind a part-glassed partition inside the bay. Situated on the southern side of the road, the Duke of Cornwall was in that block between Navy Bower and Market Street. The Plymouth Breweries pub was demolished to make way for the present development in the mid-1950s.

PLYMOUTH
P**U**BS
PAST & PRESENT

DUKE STREET INN

It stood on the corner of St. John Street Ope and Duke Street, just down from the old St. John's Baptist Church on the south-side of Duke Street and was one of a handful of pubs that at one time or another graced this, one of the older streets in Devonport.

Sadly however little of it survives today. Along with the rest of this block, between John Street Ope and Monument Street, the Duke Street Inn was pulled down in the winter of 1958/59 in a move that heralded the building of the boundary wall around that part of Devonport newly annexed by the Dockyard. Before then Queen Street, which runs across the top of Cornwall Street, had run straight on into Edinburgh Road picking up James Street before continuing down to Mutton Cove. Then Duke Street was some small distance from the dockyard wall - now most of its northern side is a part of that "new" wall.

PLYMOUTH
P**U**BS
PAST & PRESENT

30

THE EMPIRE

It stood almost half-way along Cambridge Street, just before the junction with Cambridge Lane West, on the site now just inside the car park at the back of the Market - on the western side coming in from Cornwall Street. Originally a plain beerhouse, early references don't always give it a name but it was clearly known as the Empire in the late nineteenth century, the name itself being a typical patriotic Victorian one "when the British Empire was one on which the sun never sets" (Dunkling and Wright - Dictionary of Pub Names). The building itself probably dates from the early part of the nineteenth century. Elizabeth Stanbury was the licensee here throughout the 1880s and time was when there were half a dozen pubs or beerhouses in this road running from King Street to Morley Street. Sadly, although the pub (photographed here in 1935) and virtually all of the street survived the war, it did not survive the post-war planning and it was pulled down in the late 1950s.

PLYMOUTH PUBS PAST & PRESENT

31

THE FALCON

The original Falcon was built less than ten years after the open fields of Ford were first sold for development in 1855. First recorded licensee who we have knowledge of is John Collings in 1862. Collings was here a good twenty years and as such is probably the longest serving landlord the Falcon has known. In the 1930s William Waldron Tucker followed Louis Roseman here and with his wife ran the pub until April 1941 when incendiary bomb damage forced the family to move. In 1943 the licence was suspended and only restored when the pub had been successfully rebuilt in 1957.

The top photograph here shows the original Melville Road building. Incidentally there was once another Falcon in Devonport but in 1963 it was re-named the Royal Clarence. Whether the pub was named after the bird, or one of the many Royal Naval ships to bear that name, or even, as in the case of the Falcon in Bude, after a stagecoach that used to operate from there is unclear.

PLYMOUTH
P**U**BS
PAST & PRESENT

FAMOUS FIRKIN

Long known as the Adelaide Inn, through its location on the corner of Adelaide Place and Adelaide Street and in turn after the bride of the Duke of Clarence, Adelaide Louisa Theresa Caroline Amelia, daughter of George the Duke of Saxe-Meiningen, this is now the Famous Firkin. The new name however has no local point of reference and is rather just one of now four Plymouth pubs to adopt the trendy and rather dubious Firkin epithet. Questionable commercial considerations rather than a genuine reference to any celebrated small, 9-gallon cask, doubtless prompted the name change here as in the other locations. Thankfully the street names remain however and the young bride of the sailor king, who was a regular visitor to the area in his youth, is still remembered in the nearby Royal Adelaide. Queen Adelaide incidentally, who was twenty-seven years younger than her husband, survived him and died when her niece Victoria had been on the throne twelve years, in 1849.

PLYMOUTH PUBS PAST & PRESENT

THE FAREHAM

The sign proclaims that this is the cosiest freehouse in Plymouth and certainly it must be just about the smallest licensed premises in the city. Situated in the Commercial Road end of Sutton Road this mid-nineteenth century pub would once have been full of all the many men employed in the Victorian dockside industries on this side of Sutton Harbour. With the fish market now on this side of the harbour and an increasingly leisure-based series of developments springing up around here, this area looks set for a new but very different era of prosperity. Sharing its name with the Hampshire town on Portsmouth Harbour, the Fareham's longest serving licensee appears to have been Edward Murch who was here from 1923 through to 1950. He in turn succeeded Thomas Murch.

Fareham incidentally means "homestead where the ferns grow" and although the name comes here from Hampshire it's nevertheless interesting to note that a near neighbour - the Thistle Park Tavern takes its name from a field of thistles that was here before this part of town was developed.

PLYMOUTH
P**UBS**
PAST & PRESENT

THE FELLOWSHIP

The Fellowship Inn in Trevithick Road is but a few yards from the ancient Plymouth to Saltash Road and just a short distance from that high point in King's Tamerton where there was once believed to have been a Roman signal station (hence the comparatively recent local street names Roman Way and Roman Road).

When it was first opened in 1940 that route to Saltash was still being used by many ferry users and, from 1961 onwards, by the many users of the Tamar Road Bridge. Still a busy route, it has been somewhat quieter since the Parkway opened and while the Fellowship remains the only pub in King's Tamerton today it's interesting to note that before the war there was an old time hostelry, the Traveller's Rest, run by the Deacon family adjoining their smithy, just a little way down the hill in Weston Mill Road.

One of comparatively few pubs of its period in Plymouth, the Fellowship shares certain architectural features with its contemporaries, the Cherry Tree and the Golden Hind, where current landlord David Read recently spent some time.

PLYMOUTH
P▮BS
PAST & PRESENT

THE FERRYBOAT

A logical enough place for a pub, just up from the ferry crossing, the pub doesn't date from the very early days of the Torpoint Ferry because in the beginning the Devon landing point was down at North Corner. North Corner was nearer that bit of the Dockyard then in existence and there was little beyond it, hence the name North Corner. In time the crossing moved up here and the first recorded licensee we have here at what was then the Passage House Inn was Mary Hay in 1812.

Known in later years as the Ferry Point Inn, then the Ferry Hotel and Coach Builders Arms, the pub is today known as the Ferryboat. In recent years it has had quite a succession of licensees but from 1940 through to 1976 it was in the hands of first Francis then Muriel Tunstall.

FLORA INN

One hundred years ago there were four beerhouses in Flora Street, one of them, No.36, housing the Flora Inn, which was then run by James Bolt. Standing opposite the junction with the long gone Granby Street, just down from King Street (Flora Street then running between Union Street and King Street) the pub clearly took it's name from the mid-nineteenth century thoroughfare it stood in. The street in turn was named in honour of the abundance of flora and fauna that grew in John Rendell's neighbouring nursery, a major feature of the area, opened amid great festivities in 1850 - although Rendell had been trading here many years before that. Sadly the blitz hit this area quite badly and almost all of Flora Street has been redeveloped, with the Western Approach car park now to the east of it. (Note the lamp-post in both pictures).

PLYMOUTH
P▢BS
PAST & PRESENT

37

FORD HOTEL

In 1855 the area known as Ford, one of the few pieces of freehold land left in the borough, was put on the market and readily bought up by the Devon and Cornwall Freehold Land Society. One of the first premises to be completed on the new estate was the Ford Hotel ... it was also the first licensed house to be re-built in Plymouth after it had been completely destroyed in the bombing of 1941. Out of commission for thirteen years, it was the Octagon Brewery who were responsible for re-instating this hillside hotel, which stands at the western end of Alexandra Road. Clearly it takes its name from the estate on which it stands, which in turn was named after the erstwhile crossing of Keyham Lake at the bottom what became Ford Hill. When Ford was first laid out in the middle of last century Keyham Lake would have come as far inland as the top of St. Levan Road and the "ford" would have been the most westerly pedestrian crossing point.

PLYMOUTH
P■BS
PAST & PRESENT

FRANCIS ARMS

One of Plymouth's smaller public houses the Francis Arms manages to retain much of the indigenous character of a corner pub built to service the new housing development it was a part of, that is between King Street and Wyndham Square, an area laid out in the late nineteenth century.

Elizabeth Crane then T.F. Trebilco were among the early licensees here, while William Swain was here just after the First World War when this was a New Victoria Brewery pub. Later sold to Ind Coope, the longest serving post-war licensee was Charles Wells, who was here when peace was declared and who stayed until 1953 - although later, Ken, then Joyce Hawke saw the Francis through from 1966 to 1984.

PLYMOUTH PUBS PAST & PRESENT

39

FREEMASON'S ARMS

No. 26 John Street, Devonport, was the address of this Freemason's Arms, one of three in the Three Towns, the others being in Chapel Street, Stonehouse and at Cattedown, Plymouth.

Strickly speaking though this was in Morice Town rather than Devonport, between Tamar Road and Ferry Road, part of the Dockyard's Albert Gate clearly visible to the left here. John Street survives today, its northern side demolished to make way for the bridge connecting Morice Yard with Keyham Yard, built in the mid-1950s. John Williamson is the earliest licensee we have record of here. He was landlord in the 1820s when Devonport was still booming after its great expansion during the Napoleonic Wars.

PLYMOUTH PUBS PAST & PRESENT

40

THE FRIENDSHIP

The Friendship was probably built sometime in the 1840s and James Wiblin is recorded as one of its earliest licensees in 1852. Furthermore the pub almost certainly owes its name to the street it stands in Amity Place - amity and friendship - the two terms are virtually interchangeable. Quite why the street was called Amity Place however is less than clear, particularly as the neighbouring streets - Waterloo, Wellington, Nelson and Armada - built around the same time, all have quite logical local explanations. Indeed there are similarly named streets in Stoke Damerel, and in Morice Town, in Albert Road, there is another, almost contemporary, Friendship pub. Such names were popular in the nineteenth century, as was the sentimental imagery that frequently accompanied the name on the pub sign. Here today however we find a ship, a Friendship, which, given the nautical connection of some of the other local names, begs the question was there an important naval ship called the Amity? The answer is that by 1800 there had been three, but nothing obviously significant locally and so we can but wonder.

PLYMOUTH
PUBS
PAST & PRESENT

GOLDEN HIND

In 1938 Plymouth won a boundary extension which saw the city's acreage suddenly jump from 5,711 to 9,595; new housing estates were begun inside the re-aligned city limits and three pubs were built - the Cherry Tree, the Fellowship and the Golden Hind.

A licence was issued and the work began that year and in 1939 Bob Warren became the pub's first landlord, staying here throughout the war, until 1947, when Samuel Morrell, in whose name the licence here was first issued, took over for three years.

Probably the most notable landlord here arrived in 1959. After a couple of years at the Duke of York in Tavistock and ten years with Plymouth Argyle, that man was the Welsh international goalkeeper Bill Shortt who made over 350 appearances for the Pilgrims before spending 26 years at the helm of the Golden Hind.

It is one of the few pubs in Plymouth today nominally associated with the life of Drake, in this instance the re-christened ship in which he made his epic voyage of circumnavigation.

PLYMOUTH PUBS PAST & PRESENT

GREYHOUND INN

It operated as a pub until early 1983 in Millbay Road and is now essentially the accommodation element of the new expansive red brick pub - Sippers - that has been tacked on alongside it.

In later years this was a lone survivor in this particular stretch of road, between the wars and before that however this was a busy stretch boasting half a dozen hostelries.

In addition to the Greyhound there was the Brunel, Bosphorous, Terminus, South Devon and Ocean Mail. In those happier times the Greyhound was a family pub, run by Jack Millard, then his brother-in-law Thompson Moss, followed by his son, Tom Moss, who was here until he was called up in 1940.

Joseph Perriam was licensee here back in the 1850s when the railway had just arrived and Millbay was a much busier place. One hundred years later the character had changed, the railway had gone and now with the Brittany Ferries Terminal in Millbay Docks, Sippers on this site, and the Pavilions across the road, the area bears little resemblance to its nineteenth century appearance.

PLYMOUTH
P BS
PAST & PRESENT

43

HACKNEY CARRIAGE

Although the Octagon was first laid out in the 1820s it would appear that the buildings there were originally all rather grand private residences. By the 1850s however the surrounding area had become extensively built up and the character of the Octagon began to change. S. Chubb, here in the 1860s, is the first licensee we can find record of in 74 Union Street and among his nineteenth century successors were Michael Sullivan and Samuel Nottle. By Nottle's time the pub was known as the Antelope, whether it had always been known by that name is unclear; although the name is common enough it could perhaps be that here it is not an heraldic reference to the Duke of Gloucester or, more likely locally, the Duke of Bedford, but rather a reference to the torpedo gunboat - *Antelope* - launched in Devonport Dockyard in July 1893.

Whatever the history of that particular name though for the last ten years or so the pub has been known as the Hackney Carriage. Generally taken today to refer to any kind of taxi the original Hackney Carriage was a motorless wooden affair pulled by a "hackney", a type of horse used in harness. It is this, more typically Victorian, mode of transport that is, somewhat appropriately, depicted on the sign for this Victorian Plymouth public house.

PLYMOUTH
P&BS
PAST & PRESENT

HAM STREET VAULTS

This pub stood at the bottom of the present Hampton Street, in the middle, where there is now a traffic island at the side of Charles Cross Police Station.

Originally it was in Ham Street (later absorbed into Ebrington Street), on the corner of the erstwhile southern section of Gibbon Street.

Its last owners were Allied Breweries who took over from Ind Coope. Prior to that it was for a time in the hands of the New Victoria Brewery in Weston Park Road. Known as Symons Wine & Spirit Vaults in 1847, it was then run by HJ Symons. A distinctive, if not unusual building, it was closed on October 28, 1972, and demolished three weeks later.

PLYMOUTH
P▌BS
PAST & PRESENT

HAMPTON COURT INN

The Duke of Clarence, the Sailor King - William IV, was quite possibly the most popular "Royal" Plymouth has ever known. In his younger days he was a frequent visitor to the area and each of the Three Towns named a street in his honour - but whereas Stonehouse and Devonport still have their Clarence Place, Plymouth's Clarence Street has long since disappeared and with it the Hampton Court Inn. Running between the original Old Town Street and Gibbon Street it's path took it straight through that site now occupied by the College of Art, indeed part of the road ran more or less along the gap between the two blocks at the rear of the tower block. The Hampton Court Inn itself was originally a private residence, No.4 Clarence Street and became a beerhouse sometime in the 1870s or 1880s. Notable for the number of women who held its license, Mrs. Adelaide Miller and Mrs. Caroline Spettigue were among the early landladies, the inn's name doubtless had more to do with the original Hampton Street, which it ran into, than the Palace created for Cardinal Wolsey in the early sixteenth century.

PLYMOUTH
P▪BS
PAST & PRESENT

HEATH'S HOTEL

In 1882 Cousin's Hotel Buffet was redecorated we are told, in "delicate salmon tints" and was given an elegant marbled bar counter. As the 1940s dawned this was still known as Cousin's but then in February 1945 an advertisement in the Herald announced that henceforth the Hotel would be exclusively for men and that it would be known as the Bodega. The sign to the right here on this 1950s photograph shows the Bodega Bar - the name apparently comes from a Spanish word referring to a cellar or shop where only wine is sold.

In 1949 the building, one of the last George Street survivors, was compulsorily purchased by the Council and throughout the fifties Heath's Hotel, as it now was, was leased out to the Starkey, Knight and Ford Brewery. It closed in November 1958.

THE HERBERT

Not that long after the development of the Keyham Steam Yard and the extension of what was then called the Cornwall Railway through Morice Town, there was a major housing development programme to the west of Navy Row (Albert Road). Among the new streets thus formed was Herbert Street, leading down from a newly-built bridge over the railway. Herbert is the family name of the Earls of Caernarvon, who were major landowners in the westcountry and the Herbert Hotel is one of at least two British pubs named in their honour - there is also the Herbert Arms in Chirbury, Clwyd.

One of the remarkable features of this distinctive Devonport hostelry is the small number of licensees it has had over the years, many of whom have been remarkably long-serving.

PLYMOUTH
P**U**BS
PAST & PRESENT

HILL PARK HOTEL

Hill Park Crescent was one of the first terraces in this area to be constructed and as the name implies this would have been a long and curved row of buildings on the edge of a hill next to a large green open space or park. Appropriately enough one of the first, if not the first landlord of the Hill Park Hotel was a Mr. Greenfield. Back then, in the middle of the nineteenth century, there were green fields all around and Greenbank was still green too. The old Greenbank Prison (later used as a Police Station and then by the Health Service) was completed, just down from here, in1849. There is a suggestion that the Prison Governor lived here for some years - hence the observational tower at the top.

By the 1880s the area had been fairly heavily built up and today apart from Freedom Fields Park nearby you have to travel some distance to find any undeveloped land.

PLYMOUTH PUBS PAST & PRESENT

HYDE PARK HOTEL

It hasn't always been on an island and it appears to have been built in the garden of an earlier hostelry - the Townsend Inn. Servington Lethbridge appears to have been the last known licensee of the Townsend and first references to the Hyde Park Hotel, Mutley appear in the 1860s. For many years all traffic was directed around this side of the pub and unless turning off into Hyde Park Road itself, carried on up Townsend Hill.

The landlord here as the Hyde Park in all probability celebrated its centenary was Alex Govan who came to the pub after finishing his footballing career at Plymouth Argyle (he played 145 games for the club between 1946 and 1960 and scored 35 goals).

PLYMOUTH
P**BS
PAST & PRESENT

INDIAN INN

Undoubtedly one of the more unusual pub names in Plymouth is the Indian Inn at Stoke. The Indian motif used to be a popular one with tobacconists who typically displayed a sign showing a Red Indian, complete with full head-dress, either holding a pipe or a tobacco leaf. However the current sign of this unassuming hostelry, which barely stands out from the terrace of housing it stands in, just shows the head of an Indian, without any reference to smoking and the origin of the name remains lost in the mists of time. Trading as the Indian since the 1850s at least, Vasco Antonio Gomez was one of the early, long-serving, licensees here, and he was followed, although not immediately, by George Gomez, in 1890.

PLYMOUTH PUBS PAST & PRESENT

JAMES STREET VAULTS

The foundations of James Street were laid in the first quarter of the nineteenth century although it was to take some twenty years before it had been fully developed. Quite why it is called James Street is unclear, but whatever the explanation it is quite likely linked with the explanation of the naming of the neighbouring John Street - sons of the developer responsible for part of the construction of this area? Whatever the origins of the street name and therefore that of the pub, we find, among the various licensees here in the nineteenth century Messrs. Greenfield, Magenis and Curzon (who was here throughout the 1890s). This century two men have dominated the records of this pub; Robert Evens, here from 1933 through to 1956, and Leslie Mills, who succeeded Evens' widow Alice in 1961, and who stayed here until 1984.

PLYMOUTH PUBS PAST & PRESENT

JUBILEE INN

At one time there were two Jubilees in Plymouth. Now there are none. One was in Old Town Street and was renamed the Telegraph, soon after Queen Victoria's jubilee. The other was here at the northern end of what was Jubilee Street (now part of Sutton Road).

Jubilee Street was named in honour of the new Eastern road and the building of the Embankment, commemorating George III's jubilee in 1809. It had nothing to do with Queen Victoria, as suggested by the pub sign. Built as the Jubilee Hotel, it was opened in 1835, two years before Victoria came to the throne. Brent, Clatworthy, Swan, Anderson and Langridge are among the names of its 19th century licensees, and prior to its being a Whitbread hostelry, the Jubilee was in the hands of Starkey, Knight and Ford Brewery. In January 1981 it ceased trading, and was pulled down soon afterwards to allow Exeter Street to be widened.

**PLYMOUTH
P✦BS
PAST & PRESENT**

KEPPEL'S HEAD

In 1978 John and Rosa Scott bought this former beerhouse/ciderhouse and when the adjoining corner site was later acquired, the premises were extended into what is now known as the Complex. The area inside known as the Gentleman's Retreat is effectively the old Keppel's Head; the old sign, now illuminated, is still in the pub, the old bottle and jug door, now panelled over, is also still there and outside, on the Keyham Road elevation, the brown tiles we see in this mid-fifties picture are still there under a coat of white paint. There were two Admiral Keppels who were familiar to Plymouth, one helped Joshua Reynolds with a free passage to Italy in the mid-eighteenth century the other, Admiral Sir Henry Keppel, who the pub was almost certainly named after, was Commander-in-Chief, Devonport in the 1870s.

PLYMOUTH
P▪BS
PAST & PRESENT

KEYHAM WINE AND SPIRIT VAULTS

It's not exactly in Keyham and it doesn't exactly look much like this anymore but although it's been rebuilt the name has survived. Today the lively Keyham Inn stands on this site on the corner of Albert Road and Charlotte Street the building here having been demolished in the mid-1960s. The story goes that part of the pub actually fell down and that there were regulars in here drinking when it happened.

The original building was probably one of the earliest pubs to be built in Albert Road, back in the days when it was Navy Row. The earliest licensee we have record of was Sarah Wicks who was here in 1844 when plans were already under way for the building of the new Keyham Steam Yard. Of the subsequent licensees, two, Richard Maynard and his successor Harry Ferraro have served here thirty years - either side of 1905.

PLYMOUTH
P**U**BS
PAST & PRESENT

LITTLE MUTTON MONSTER

Built at the beginning of the nineteenth century and known for many years as the Blue Anchor this Mutton Cove pub became the Naval Inn around 1857 and then, in the early 1890s, the New Pier Inn. This third name was to last almost one hundred years but then, in July 1990, it changed again to the Little Mutton Monster.

The "new pier" of the 1890s was a reference to the T-shaped pier constructed off the earlier stoneworks of Mutton Cove, while the Little Mutton Monster is a reference to the dog "Monster" which belongs to the co-owner and joint licensee of the pub and who formed the Little Monster Property Company to buy the pub five years ago.

PLYMOUTH PUBS PAST & PRESENT

LORD HOOD

It stood on the corner of Cannon Street and King Street and is now buried under the new flat developments that have obliterated King Street and seen part of it renamed Granby Way. King Street itself was probably laid out sometime in the early eighteenth century, around the 1730s, but whether the pub was that old is not clear. Certainly the name wasn't. The Lord Hood in question was undoubtedly the Dorset-born Samuel Hood (1724-1810) who was made Viscount Hood (Lord Hood) in 1796. Nelson served under him and considered him the ablest of our Admirals in the early years of the war with France. From a famous seafaring family, Hood's brother, Alexander (1727-1814), also had a distinguished naval career and was made Viscount Bridport in 1801.

One of the earliest licenseees we have record of at the Lord Hood was William Hocken who saw out the last years of the Napoleonic War behind this bar. Pinhey, Knowling, Frost, Uglow and Vercoe were among the early nineteenth century landlords who followed him here.

PLYMOUTH
P**U**BS
PAST & PRESENT

MARKET HOUSE INN

With three doors onto Market Street, Stonehouse, the substantial Market House Inn stood just yards away from the former Edgcumbe Street - later absorbed into Union Street and now Edgcumbe Street again. South of Union Street and on the eastern side of Market Street, the inn was not far from the site of the old Stonehouse Market, which for the greater part of the nineteenth century occupied a large site at the northern end of Market Street. The street itself then ran from High Street to Caroline Place crossing what was George Street and is now part of Stonehouse Street, on its way. Redevelopment of the area in the 1970s broke up the line of the street and led to the demolition of the pub which had been structurally upgraded in the post war years.

PLYMOUTH
P*BS
PAST & PRESENT

MILITARY ARMS

The Military Arms, No.116 Fore Street, stood on the corner of Fore Street and what was Princess Street Ope, and what became High Street. The Electric Theatre, formerly the Devonport Public Hall, stood on the opposite corner.

Like so much of the street this was destroyed in the 1941 Blitz and, sadly, today there is nothing left of this part of the street.

The name itself was an obvious enough one, the pub and the name dated back at least to the days of the Napoleonic Wars - William Rowe was licensee here in 1812 - and then there were thousands of soldiers stationed in the town and one of the main barracks, Granby Barracks, was just at the top of High Street.

PLYMOUTH
PUBS
PAST & PRESENT

MUTLEY TAVERN

Question: What is the connection between the Railway Hotel, built in the 1860s in Zetland Place and the Mutley Tavern that stands today in Furzehill Road?

Answer: They are one and the same building.

Zetland Place was developed in the mid-1860s at the southern end of what had long since been known as Furze Hill Lane. Before Alexandra Road was laid out this was the principal route from North Hill to Lipson. A situation that persisted for sometime after the railway had cut a fresh path through this bit of countryside and under Mutley Plain. Situated just minutes away from Mutley Station (which closed in 1939) the Railway Hotel was a logical enough name for this substantial house and interestingly enough the first licensee here was also a builder, so was it he, John Hyne, who was responsible for its construction? One hundred years ago, when Oliver Rattle was licensee here, there were over 30 Railway Inns or Hotels in Devon, today that number has depleted by one at least as, for the last ten years or so, this hostelry has been known as the Mutley Tavern.

PLYMOUTH
P BS
PAST & PRESENT

NEWTOWN HOTEL

Variously listed over the years as being either in York Street or Cobourg Street, the Newtown Inn stood on the western junction of those two major thoroughfares and would appear to have been built in the first quarter of the nineteenth century

Much of the original, pre-war housing in this area, south of what is now North Cross roundabout, would have been constructed about this time, hence the name Newtown Inn.

William Menhneir was probably one of the first licensees here and records indicate that he ran, and doubtless owned, this pub as long ago as 1823.

The last private owner of the Newtown was Leslie Barry, who first came here in 1922 and was here in the early years of the war, until 1941.

Like the Oporto opposite the Newtown it survived the Blitz, but eventually the grand old Starkey, Knight and Ford pub was pulled down to make way for road improvements in the late 1960s.

PLYMOUTH
P**U**BS
PAST & PRESENT

NOAH'S ARK

Two hundred years ago if you had found yourself standing just outside the north-eastern door of Boots the Chemist in Old Town Street you would have been right on the edge of town at the Old Town Gate.

Beyond it - just a handful of buildings, a few odd houses and nothing else of consequence until you got to Compton.

Among that group of houses, standing 30 yards or so to the north of the gate was the Noah's Ark. Rebuilt in the 1890s we see here the original pub, one of two nineteenth century pubs of that name in Plymouth (the other was on the Barbican) and the one that is the antecedent of the post-war Noah's Ark built several hundred yards away in Courtenay Street.

Its first address was Old Town Without, later it became No.2 Saltash Street.

PLYMOUTH
P▪BS
PAST & PRESENT

THE NOTTE INN

You could be forgiven for thinking that this is one of Plymouth's newer pubs, as in many ways it is ... but in other ways it isn't. It was in June 1993 that what was Chambers Wine Bar became the Notte Inn public house. It had previously been the Lourdes Bistro, amongst other things, and before that even the Plymouth Varnish and Colour Company Limited, Varnish Manufacturers.

The Varnish Company arrived here, at No.60 Notte Street, sometime around 1923, and interestingly enough if we go back before that we find that this building was in fact a pub - the Yarmouth Inn.

Earliest reference to it appears to be about 1870. It seems that Notte Street was redeveloped around this time and it is likely that No.60 Notte Street was first opened as a pub.

Sometime around 1914, incidentally, the Yarmouth Inn became the Yarmouth Hotel, Thomas Hoyle and his Sons were then running the place.

PLYMOUTH
P*BS
PAST & PRESENT

63

THE NOTTINGHAM

By the middle of the nineteenth century Plymouth had almost developed as far as the line of the new South Devon Railway that passed under Mutley Plain, although most of the land north of North Road East was still open fields. Apart from some isolated development along Tavistock Road this was truly the north road of the town. One exception to this though could be found at the junction of Mutley Plain and Greenbank Road (then called Prison Road because of the newly built gaol there), for here we found, beyond Hill Park Crescent and Alton Terrace, two short terraces of housing - Chester Place and Nottingham Place. The two blocks formed a wide angled "L" shape - each leg of the "L" ending where it met the Plymouth Leat. In the corner of that "L" was "The Nottingham", then the most northern hostelry in Plymouth.

Although possibly not the first licensee here, B.E. Cotton, who was the landlord in 1857, is certainly a likely candidate for that title. Like his many successors here though he didn't stay very long and Laskey, Hawke, Rickard and Clatworthy are just a few of the names that went above the front door here before the turn of the century.

PLYMOUTH
P▮BS
PAST & PRESENT

NOWHERE INN

When first opened in the first half of the nineteenth century this unassuming beerhouse in Gilwell Street could justifiably have been said to have been on the road to nowhere - there was little or no development beyond the new houses that had sprung up in what had been Gibbon's Field. Sherwell House and, according to the evidence of at least one map, Gilwell House stood to the north and east, but there was little else. 150 years later, although this pub is now nearer the very heart of old Plymouth rather than being on the edge of town, the Nowhere still finds itself somewhat tucked away, standing as it does opposite the former dairy which for many long years occupied part of the former grounds of Gilwell House. Quite why it's called the Nowhere no-one seems exactly sure although according to a piece of correspondence from the old Plymouth Breweries "When a husband was asked by his wife where he had been, and he did not wish her to know he had been to the pub, he could truthfully reply - 'Nowhere'." (Coincidentally, or maybe not, Plymouth is also blessed with a No Place Inn)

Quite when this wag is supposed to have drunk here is less than clear, so we don't know which landlord was responsible for perpetuating the joke, but we do know that there have been more than thirty changes of licensee here in the last seventy years and that none of them have been here longer than six and a half years. Indeed the last one here longer than that was John Skinner at the turn of the century.

PLYMOUTH
P▢BS
PAST & PRESENT

THE OFFICE

Originally known as the Royal Naval Hospital Tavern, or more simply the Hospital, this pub was renamed in the early 1980s by a group that were planning to open a chain of Offices around the country. The current licensees, Dee and Peter Lloyd have since considered changing it back, but they say the locals have all got used to it, and so have the taxi drivers and they feel that it's perhaps now gone on too long to change it again.

A popular local hostelry the Office was long a favourite haunt with those working in and visiting the old Royal Naval Hospital the gate of which it stands alongside. Work on the Hospital began in the 1750s and it is thought that the pub was built in what became High Street, Stonehouse, not that long afterwards.

PLYMOUTH
P▮BS
PAST & PRESENT

OLD RING OF BELLS

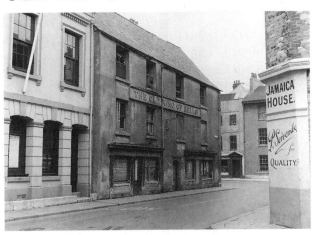

Had the "Old Ring of Bells" not been pulled down in January 1957 it could well have been a contender for the oldest tavern in Plymouth today. Sadly, however, the building had been derelict for a number of years prior to the fifties and had ceased trading as an inn back on December 16, 1922.

Thought to have been built some time around 1580, it stood on the corner of Woolster Street where it turns into Vauxhall Street. Demolished at the same time were two former hostelries fronting onto Vauxhall Street immediately around this corner, known in the nineteenth century as the "Steam Packet" and the "Prince George". The latter, like the "Ring of Bells" had many sixteenth century features, including an Elizabethan plaster ceiling.

The old line of this corner has now, of course, gone as the road here has been widened and given much more of a curve. George Lidstone was the last licensee and had been here more than a decade when the pub called time in 1922.

PLYMOUTH PUBS PAST & PRESENT

THE OPORTO

An earlier pub on this site appears to have been called the Morning Star, but for some reason it had been restyled the Oporto Wine Vaults by the 1890s. It would then appear to have been altogether rebuilt in the mid-1930s. A blitz survivor it stood for some years in splendid isolation at the top of York Street, a little down from and almost opposite the Albion and the Newtown.

A Pops - or Popplestone & Co - House, the Oporto was one of six such establishments in Plymouth at one time. By no means unique, there is another Oporto in London, the pub almost certainly takes its name from the original name for port - the famous strong dark-red wine from Portugal. Port is quite simply a shortened form of O Porto, a reference to the city and seaport in Northern Portugal, the chief port for shipment of wines from that country. Porto is also known as Oporto and was even for a time known to us as Port O Porto.

PLYMOUTH
P**U**BS
PAST & PRESENT

PICKEN'S WINE VAULTS

It stood on the northern side of Whimple Street, just along from the Western National offices and William's café.

Substantially refurbished at the beginning of the twentieth century - the date AD 1906 is visible above the gable and windows - the Wine Vaults, with its six-day licence, was finally closed in mid-1950s, around the time this photograph was taken.

It was privately owned by William Adams, of Princess Square, as late as the 1920s. George Picken (1933-38) was the only licensee of that name in the later years of the building's life.

Thomas Hannibal Penwill was the landlord here when time was finally called in September 1954. The site can easily be identified today by the corner of the Royal Assurance building, clearly visible here and still under construction to the right of Picken's. It runs at right angles to Whimple Street and the site of the old licensed premises is now clear as roadway.

PLYMOUTH
P▢BS
PAST & PRESENT

PORTLAND INN

On the corner of James Street and Portland Place West stood a small early nineteenth century beerhouse, the Portland Inn. George Kent was licensee here in 1850 and 100 years later, not long before it closed, Adelaide Julia Welbore Ellis was the licensee. Mrs. Ellis's husband Albert had taken over here just after war had been declared at the end of 1939. In 1941 Adelaide married a Mr. Forshaw but kept the licence in her (new) name, ten years later however she changed her name by deed poll and became Mrs. Ellis once more. In 1953 Walter Venning, who was to be the last licensee, took over this typical, small, Plymouth street-corner pub, which closed in 1956. Little today survives of the original James Street, which is now right in the middle of the Plymouth University campus. The road which linked Cobourg Street with North Road East however still contains the other old pub - the James Street Vaults.

PLYMOUTH
P**U**BS
PAST & PRESENT

70

POST OFFICE INN

According to Worth it was not until 1793 that a Post Office was established in Devonport, and not until 1814 that we have any clue as to the location of such a place - and that was Fore Street. We can only wonder therefore about the Post Office Inn in Market Street. Thomas Ebdon was its licensee in 1798 and as there is no reason to suppose that he was the first. Perhaps, like many other Post Office Inns around the country, this was originally named because it provided post office facilities, before there was a recognised Post Office in Plymouth Dock - as it was then.

William Webber, William Bickell and Bithiah Head are among the other early landlords here, while Harold Wilson was among the last. Meanwhile 100 years ago John Popplestone was the licensee of this one time Popplestone's Brewery pub, which was demolished in the mid-fifties when the dockyard expanded.

PLYMOUTH
P**BS
PAST & PRESENT

PRINCE ALFRED

Prince Alfred, or "Affie" as he was apparently known to the rest of his family, was born in 1844, around the time, in all probability, that this beerhouse was opened in Clarence Place, Stonehouse. He was the fourth child and second son of Queen Victoria and Prince Albert and at one time almost became the King of Greece. Given the title of Duke of Edinburgh, he came to Plymouth on a number of occasions over the years before his death in 1900 - indeed it was he who laid the foundation stone for the rebuilding of Smeaton's Tower on the Hoe in 1882.

Florence Bishop was licensee of the Prince Alfred in 1960 when it received a publican's grant and thereby ceased to be just a beerhouse.

PLYMOUTH
P**BS
PAST & PRESENT

PRINCE OF WALES

Union Terrace, Morice Town was the original address for this Prince of Wales, back in the days when each of the Three Towns had its own pub of that name (indeed it is traditionally one of the more popular pub names - at one time there were nearly 100 in Greater London alone). Later Union Terrace became Martin Terrace and it is now part of Keyham Road. Like the other two local Prince of Wales pubs, however, this one is no longer operating, although the building still stands. The licence here was surrendered in November 1992 and the pub has been closed since. Built, it would appear, in the first ten years or so after Keyam Steam Yard itself was built, J. Gregory is the first licensee we have record of in the early 1860s. Cedric Emmett was here for fouteen years before the last war but the longest serving licensee here appears to have been one of the last, Coleen Fry, who came to the Prince of Wales in May 1967 and was around to celebrate fifteen years here in 1982.

PLYMOUTH
P◻BS
PAST & PRESENT

PROSPECT INN

Prospect Place still runs between Citadel Road and Walker Terrace but it no longer is home to those wartime survivors that were cleared in the late-fifties, early-sixties to make way for the then new Mayflower Hotel and multi-storey accommodation development at the southern end.

In 1940 Robert Gully was in Prospect Villa alongside his Millbay Park Garage at one end and Archie Bussell was at No.9, The Prospect Inn, two doors along from Archibald Trelawney's shop.

Bussell was succeeded Arthur Howard who was here until 1952 when the licence was removed to the Old Road Inn, Laira. The name itself undoubtedly comes from the villa which also gave its name to the street and which would have commanded a fine view, or prospect, when first built.

RED LION

This unassuming public house, closed in 1961 and demolished soon after, stood on the eastern side of Cambridge Street which ran north-south across part of the western side of the modern city centre. The pub site itself is roughly where the junction of Mayflower Street and Western Approach now is, just below the traffic island.

For many years there were two Red Lions in the Three Towns (the other was in Stonehouse) today there are none ... however it is still the most common pub name in Britain - there are over 600 nationwide. John of Gaunt, the most powerful man in England for much of the fourteenth century, inspired most of the early pubs of this name, while in the early years of the seventeenth century James I (James VI of Scotland) made his contribution by ordering that a heraldic red lion should be displayed in all public places.

PLYMOUTH PUBS PAST & PRESENT

THE REVENUE

It stood on the corner of Duke Street and Tavistock Road; a modest four-storey building with an unusually imposing entrance for a public house, this was the Revenue Hotel ... although at first glance one might forgive the uninitiated for thinking it was called the Double Diamond. Offering "Commercial Accommodation" for the best part of 100 years, it was first recorded as the Revenue Inn back in the 1860s - the building was, just a decade before that, the local Inland Revenue Office. This doubtless accounts for the imposing entrance as well as, of course, the name of the hotel. Situated just a few doors down from the Harvest Home, at one time in the 1860s both hostelries were in the hands of the same family - the Hamleys - but that appears to be the only time the two were linked. Harold Darlington, the last licensee here also appears to have been the longest serving. Pulled down in the re-vamping of Drake's Circus, the site of the Revenue is buried beneath the Roundabout itself, at the top of the road coming up from Charles Church.

PLYMOUTH
P**BS
PAST & PRESENT

ROSE AND CROWN

Before this part of Devonport was redeveloped in the late 50s and early 60s, there stood, on the south eastern corner of the junction of Pembroke Street with Canterbury Street, the Rose and Crown.

The name itself is a very common one; there are over sixty in London alone and time was when there was a very famous one in Old Town Street, but the one we see here was the last of that name in the Three Towns.

While the Plymouth pub was thought to be a relic of the War of the Roses - it stood for over 300 years - the pub here probably dated back to the Napoleonic War period, although the first licensee we have record of was William Gist, in 1830.

Before the Second World War, incidentally, Pembroke Street had eight such corner pubs and a handful of others; the Albion Hotel stood directly opposite the Rose and Crown.

PLYMOUTH
P**UBS**
PAST & PRESENT

ROYAL NAVAL ARMS

By the time the Royal Naval Barracks were occupied for the first time, in 1891, out in what was then almost all open countryside beyond Keyham Steam Yard, the Royal Naval Arms, just down from the barracks gates, was already open for business. At that time though there was little else in the way of housing in area apart from Johnston Terrace.

William Bosworthick, grocer and beer retailer, was the first licensee here and, but for a brief spell between 1907-1911, there was a Bosworthick here through until 1928.

Although perhaps an obvious sounding name there doesn't appear to be many, if any, similarly named pubs in Britain, although there is the Naval and Military Arms in Gosport, and there are a number of "Navy's" around - notably on the Barbican and in Truro and Penzance.

PLYMOUTH PUBS PAST & PRESENT

SALUTATION INN

In the wake of the Crusades there were many mediaeval English inns known as the Salutation and it is interesting to note that this particular Salutation was one of the oldest inns in Stillman Street, itself an ancient Barbican thoroughfare first mentioned in 1412. A reference to the Annunciation, the greeting and proclamation of the Archangel Gabriel to the Virgin Mary, it is also noteworthy that that part of Stillman Street was once known as Seven Stars Lane, another popular name with religious overtones much used in the middle ages.

Many Salutations however did not last past Puritan times and were renamed, this one though stood almost until the very end of the nineteenth century. It was pulled down sometime around 1897 by which time most of the northern side of the street had undergone major alterations. Today there is only one old house left in the street and that dates back no further than the early nineteenth century. The basic street line however has been preserved, although it is quite a bit wider today than it was when this shot was taken. The picture, incidentally, probably dates from the early 1890s when, as the Salutation Vaults, it was run, as can be just made out on the bottom sign, by the Roach family.

79

SHIP INN

LICENSEES

1857 **James Bennett**
1867 **John Pinhey**
1880 **J. Clark**
1895 **George Dalley**
1905 **H.W. Rendell**
1921 **James Helson**
1929 **Henry Neale**
1932 **Frederick Martin**
1945 **Arthur Howard**
1945 **Leonard Ward**
1949 **Albert Moore**
1951 **Leslie Taylor**

Demolished sometime around 1960, the Ship stood in Millbay Road, between the junctions with Martin Street and Bath Street, about four doors away from Bath Street. It was, for most of its time just a beerhouse. Indeed in 1949 the licensee was fined £6 for selling whisky and ordered to pay an extra three guineas costs.

Originally this thoroughfare was known as Buckingham Place and it carried on into Mount Pleasant. Not long after work began on developing Millbay Docks however the two roads were united as Millbay Road. One hundred years ago with the docks and the railway thriving there were many watering holes dotted along the length of Millbay Road, not all of them selling alcohol for curiously enough there were five temperance hotels here in addition to the three licensed hotels, four beerhouses and one inn - namely the Greyhound where part of Sippers now stands.

PLYMOUTH
P BS
PAST & PRESENT

SIR FRANCIS DRAKE

Despite being hailed as one of Plymouth's greatest heroes (although he was born near Tavistock) there is, sadly, no pub name honouring him in Plymouth today - although there are many in other parts of the county and country. We do have the Golden Hind and the Drake's Drum though.

Until recently, vehicles could access Camden Street from the junction of Gibbon Lane and Gilwell Street and until the early seventies the first building you would have found on the northern side of Camden Street, on the corner of Mount Street, was the Sir Francis Drake. As the cockerel on the sign suggests, this was a Courage house in its later years. Prior to that it belonged to H&G Simonds, the Octagon Brewery, Starkey, Knight & Ford and, in the early 20s, the Eagle Brewery of Devonport. After well over 100 years of trading, "time" was called in the summer of '73.

PLYMOUTH
PUBS
PAST & PRESENT

81

SOMERSET ARMS

Situated on the corner of North Road West and Melbourne Street this typical late-nineteenth century pub was, until 1961, little more than a beerhouse, the change to full publicans license being effected during the time of Margaret Bodmin, the longest serving post-war licensee to date. Originally part of Densham Terrace - the signs are still in place - the pub is thought to have been built in the late 1860s, early 1870s and J. Taylor was one of the first recorded licensees here. For a while this was known as 18 Densham Terrace, then 96, then 18 again and was in what was called Higher North Road - the numbering and naming of the various sections of North Road being far from a constant matter over the years. As to the pub itself, while you will see no arms of the Somerset family outside the building, you can, at present, see two large pigs, and inside there are around 700 more. Hazel Osgood has a large collection of model porkers and it includes around 100 china pigs bought in one lot from the Queens Arms on the Barbican.

PLYMOUTH
P BS
PAST & PRESENT

SPREAD EAGLE

Although it is no longer with us it is possible to locate this pub within the context of the modern city centre, the National Westminster Bank is to the left and to the far right St. Andrew's Church. The Spread Eagle stood on the corner of what was Treville Street - running left to right - and Kinterbury Street - the narrower thoroughfare running down to the bank. It's annual licence was renewed for the last time in February 1955 and in 1957 its licence was removed to the United Services Inn at Garrison Green, Lambhay Hill. Charles Vian was landlord here in 1850 and the pub's longest serving licensee, Richard Lavis, appears to have arrived here sometime in the early 1860s and was still here 1888.

The Spread Eagle itself is a very old emblem and has been used heradically by many British families over the centuries, most of them importing the image after foreign adventures, most significantly the medieval crusades. The Spread Eagle is associated with many different countries including Austria, Germany, France, Spain, Russia and the United States of America - the Romans, however were the first to popularise the motif.

PLYMOUTH PUBS PAST & PRESENT

SUGAR REFINERY

Standing on the corner of Duke Street and Saltash Street, the early 19th century building that housed the Sugar Refinery Inn was a butcher's shop before becoming a beerhouse in about 1860.

The name came from the refinery that William Bryant and Edward James established, in nearby Mill Lane, in 1838. Bryant's brother also set up a similar concern and at one time, not long after they had sold out to the British and Irish Sugar Refining Company, in 1856, this business was paying about half of the customs receipts of the port.

The Refinery closed in 1886 but the beerhouse carried on until the 1960s when within a few years of acquiring public house status it was pulled down in the redevelopment of the Drake's Circus area.

An octagonal charity shop now stands on or near this site.

PLYMOUTH
P BS
PAST & PRESENT

THE TANDEM

Just back from the Octagon itself, on a site now occupied by a block of flats, the Tandem was No.1 Octagon Street. Records go back to at least the middle of the nineteenth century - when John Blake was the licensee - and it is likely that the Tandem started life as a pub when this part of Plymouth was first developed in the 1830s.

The pub sign on the wall here, mistakenly shows the sort of tandem we are familiar with today - the traditional bicycle made for two - but it wasn't until the late 1880s that the first tandem bicycle was ever made and the pub almost certainly took its name from the tandem harness. Used for a pair of horses pulling a gig or cart, it typified a common form of transport before motor transport dominated the highways.

Interestingly enough, the Tandem pub in Oxford dates from a similar period and there, prior to the 1840s, only one horse gigs were allowed inside the city boundary. Could it be that there was a similar ruling in Plymouth?

PLYMOUTH
P◻BS
PAST & PRESENT

TAP AND BARREL

Up until the late 1950s as you came down Ashford Road you would reach this junction and you would find only the fields and out-buildings of old Lipson Farm ahead, leaving you to follow the road around down under the railway. Then came Castleton Crescent, Ashford Close and Ashford Crescent and with it the Penguin public house. Originally a typical pub of that period it has more recently been refashioned inside and re-styled the Tap and Barrel. The new name conjuring up images of the old pub tap room where casks or barrels were "tapped" by inserting a spile-peg so that the contents could be extracted without the use of a pump. In time the tap room became the common drinking room of a pub and is effectively the ancestor of the public bar. Ironically when the Tap and Barrel acquired its new name it also lost its public bar as the new layout gave it just one long - and attractive - bar.

PLYMOUTH
PUBS
PAST & PRESENT

THE TERMINUS

For the first fifty years and more of its existence this pub, on the end of Paradise Road, Stoke, was known as the Royal Military Hospital Inn. Built just over thirty years after the Royal Naval Hospital, the Military Hospital, standing on what was then the northern bank of Stonehouse Creek, is better known today as Devonport High School for Boys. Throughout the nineteenth century though it was a hospital, however its importance diminished as civilian hospitals were built and as the role of the military in Plymouth declined. Such was the situation in the late 1870s when the London and South Western Railway created their new terminal station just below Paradise Place off King's Road. The potential custom to be attracted via the new rail link was too good to miss and so out went the old name and in came the new, and by 1880 it had become known as the Terminus. A name that it still holds today despite the fact that in the mid-1960s the station was closed down, then demolished. The new College of Further Education now stands on its site.

PLYMOUTH
P BS
PAST & PRESENT

THREE CROWNS

For the best part of 400 years it would appear that the Three Crowns has stood on the edge of Sutton Harbour, and the popular theory is that this pub, like others up and down the country, commemorates, in its name, the union of England, Wales and Scotland that became effective with the monarchy of James I in 1603. By no means all Three Crowns are interpreted in this way though and other versions include references either to the Magi, the three wise men or kings, who went to Bethlehem to visit the baby Jesus or, alternatively it is the heraldic motif of the Worshipful Company of Drapers (1364). Whatever the theory, it is interesting to note that this Barbican pub was one of three Three Crowns in the Three Towns at the beginning of the nineteenth century; the others were in Queen Street, Devonport and at "Catdown" - there was also a Three Kings in Stonehouse and a Three Cannons on the Custom House Quay.

A succession of long-serving licensees have been here since the 1920s, perhaps none more notable than the well-respected musician Monty Hunter whose distinctive Bentley was a regular feature by the side door for many years.

PLYMOUTH PUBS PAST & PRESENT

THREE FERRETS

For over a hundred years this unassuming hostelry in Charlotte Street, Devonport, was known as the Grapes Tavern. There was a time when pub names involving grapes, vines, olives and such, were far more popular than they are today. From Roman times onwards the grape motif has been used to attract those that cannot read to drinking establishments, the vine is also part of the heraldic emblem for the Worshipful Company of Distillers (est. 1638). But today breweries and publicans are aiming for a different image (with the notable exception of the Grapevine) and after this pub had stood closed for twelve months or more Rick Parker moved in and re-christened it the Three Ferrets. Interestingly enough Ferrets are just one of over 57 various subjects to be part of the Three —— style name across Britain today, three being far and away the most common number in pub names. While the name was new here, however, the entertainment was not, in as much as there has been a return to the sort of live pub entertainment of an almost cabaret/musical hall kind that the pub was once well-known for - although it's probably a little saucier today.

PLYMOUTH PUBS PAST & PRESENT

THE TIGER

Work on the Whitleigh estate began at the very dawn of the 1950s and as the layout of new housing came near to completion so this pub was opened. Built in 1958 it started trading in the first few months of 1959.

Dick and Mary Gloyne were the first couple to run the place and throughout the sixties this was a very popular new estate pub, patronised not only by the locals but also many of the officers from the former Plumer Barracks at Crownhill. Indeed the name of the pub itself is thought to have some connection with one of the Crownhill-based regiments around that time.

After an initial spell of comparatively long serving licensees - Harold Spratt was there for nine years after the Gloynes left in 1967- the Tiger has, like so many other pubs these days, gone through a fairly swift succession of licensees.

PLYMOUTH
P**U**BS
PAST & PRESENT

TRAFALGAR INN

Completely rebuilt in 1895, when this part of Ebrington Street was widened, the Trafalgar was named in honour of the famous sea-battle of 1805. News of the British victory first reached many Plymothians when an actor rushed on stage during a play, silenced the crowd and announced the success. When the cheering had subsided he raised his hand again and gave the news of Nelson's death - the cheering crowd were reduced to tears and sadness. The pub site was originally in Ham Street and only later became part of Ebrington Street itself. Since it's rebuilding 100 years ago, Cyril Phipps holds the distinction of being the longest serving licensee here. His tenancy ran from April 1930 through to February 1967, and given that there have been 18 licensees to date since, it is hard to see anyone seriously challenging that record.

PLYMOUTH PUBS PAST & PRESENT

TRELAWNY HOTEL

One hundred years ago, in 1895, Joseph Stribling bought this plot of land from General John Jago Trelawny for £157, he then borrowed £4,500 and built the Trelawny Hotel, complete with two bars, a bar parlour, club room, coach house and stables with assorted other outbuildings.

Trelawny was the owner of the whole Barne Estate and the family had been associated with the Plymouth area since Tudor times. Coincidentally the address of this Hotel was, at one time Tudor Terrace.

In 1897 Joseph Stribling died and the Octagon Brewery acquired the premises and gave a ten year lease to Harry Hearn, who appears to have stayed here just over ten years. Longest serving licensee here to date though is Bill Howett who was here from 1921 to 1939.

PLYMOUTH
P**BS**
PAST & PRESENT

TURK'S HEAD

The Turk's Head is thought to have been the oldest pub in Plymouth when it was pulled down in 1860. It was also thought that its name was a legacy of the middle ages and beyond - around the time of the Crusades (Saracen's Head and Blackamore's Head were other popular names from that period). It is possible however that although the building was very old it may not always have been a pub. That said though, there was a Turk's Head Inn in Exeter that dated from at least 1289 ... there was also a Turk's Head for many years in Devonport - but that one was much later and more likely to have taken its name from a nautical term. The Turk's Head in question here being a type of circular knot.

A great loss, much lamented at the time, the St. Andrew's Street site of the Turk's Head today and since the 1860s has been occupied by the Abbey/Kitty O'Hanlons public house.

93

THE UNITY

It would appear to be more than a coincidence that just after the old Unity on the corner of Park Street and the top end of Garden Street was pulled down as part of the improvement works around Drake's Circus in the first years of the twentieth century that a new Unity opened up here in what was then the newly rebuilt western end of Ebrington Street, just opposite what had been the bottom end of Garden Street. J.A. Batten was the first licensee here, indeed he appears to have been here before the place even had a licence. In 1896 this part of Ebrington Street (renamed Eastlake Walk after the post-war rebuilding of the Charles Street dual carriage way had divorced it from the other half of the street) had just been pulled down itself and the first occupant of the new No.21 was an Arthur Baker. Batten, who was probably the same Batten who had the Masonic Inn, Stoke at this time, succeeded him here and converted the building from whatever new use it had enjoyed to a beer house. The full pub licence came in 1940 with the removal to here of the licence of the Queens Arms in the erstwhile Densham Terrace.

PLYMOUTH
P**U**BS
PAST & PRESENT

THE UNITY

An unusual story this one ... it stood, it would appear, for a little under a hundred years and it seems only to have been a beerhouse for about half of that time. Like most beerhouses it wasn't even named in the street directories but on the original of this photograph it is just possible to make out the name of this Park Street pub - it was the Unity. Standing on the corner of Park Street and Garden Street, the date at the base of the light fitting suggests that the street was built in 1809. The photograph we can date to within a year either side of 1902 because that is when E.F. Palmer, whose name appears above the windows, was licensee here. No trace survives of Park Street today but before the war it ran approximately from east to west, from what is today the pedestrian entrance of Charles Cross Police Station to the middle of Tesco's. This end of Park Street, however, was pulled down soon after Palmer left the premises in 1903, when this end of the street was demolished to make way for the road widening, around the then new Drake's Circus, and the improvements to the bottom of Tavistock Road. The western side of Garden Street disappeared at the same time.

PLYMOUTH
P■BS
PAST & PRESENT

THE VICTORY

The Victory at Honicknowle appears, from the inn sign at least, to have been named after the flagship of Britain's great Admiral, Lord Nelson, at his finest hour - the Battle of Trafalgar in 1805. The fifth in a line of Victory's in the Royal Navy, she was laid down in 1759 and at first, because the fourth Victory had foundered in the Channel with the loss of all hands, it was almost decided not to name her thus - but in the event they went ahead anyway and six years later she was launched at Chatham. Forty years on the name proved most appropriate as the Victory, and Nelson, presided over what was probably the most decisive battle ever fought at sea - in which the combined fleets of France and Spain were vanquished without the loss of a single British ship. Nelson himself was not so fortunate and perished in that conflict. The Victory however not only survived that encounter but still survives today, immaculately preserved in Portsmouth Dockyard (about 40% of her timbers are still original).

Meanwhile this much extended, nineteenth-century inn in Farm Lane, in the heart of the modern community of Honicknowle, still enjoys a comparatively rural setting, unlike the other local pub which also commemorates that great naval encounter ... the Trafalgar in Ebrington Street.

PLYMOUTH
P■BS
PAST & PRESENT

WELCOME INN

Another victim of the post-war redevelopment of the city centre, the Welcome Inn stood on the northern side of Richmond Street, just before the corner of William Lane on a site that now lies beneath the top end of Armada Way on the south side of Mayflower Street.

Our picture shows it in June 1935, some 19 years before it was compulsorily purchased by the City Council. Norman Clarke was the last licensee here but the pub had all but closed by the time he came here and Harold Stewart, who arrived just over a year after this picture was taken, was the last licensee here for any length of time.

The name itself is a common enough one and there are many variations on the theme; Welcome Hand, Welcome Return, Welcome Sailor, Welcome Traveller, Welcome All and, perhaps the nearest now to Plymouth, the Welcome Home in Par.

**PLYMOUTH
P⬜BS
PAST & PRESENT**

THE WELLINGTON

Sir Arthur Wellesley, the 1st Duke of Wellington died at Walmer Castle, Kent in 1852 and later that year a couple of as yet unnumbered buildings were erected in the newly formed Wellington Street, Plymouth. This was a time when the Napoleonic Wars were still fresh in many memories and other new streets in the area included Trafalgar, Waterloo and Nelson. Like Nelson, Wellington had been made a Freeman of Plymouth and not surprisingly this great figure was remembered in the names of two other pubs in the area - as both Stonehouse and Devonport both had their own Wellington Inns. There was also a Wellington Hotel in Union Street, but that was named after its nineteenth century proprietor J.W. Wellington. There is incidentally a Wellington pub in Hastings that refers directly to the World War II bombers, whose pilots were trained nearby, rather than the Iron Duke himself - but that said Arthur Wellesley has the distinction of having more pubs named after him than anyone except Nelson himself. Locally though this is the only one in the Three Towns remaining. Thomas Fewins appears to have been one of the first licensees here, while William and Selina Ross have been the longest serving - over thirty years between them around the turn of the century.

PLYMOUTH
P**U**BS
PAST & PRESENT

WHICH YOU PLEASE

Here we have a rare, but by no means unique, example of an old Plymouth pub which still stands today, but which has long since ceased to be used as an alehouse of any kind - indeed it currently houses Prudence Gowns Bridal Wear. Today it boasts a very pinky interior, ten years ago, when the Bridal Wear shop first moved in, it was a typical late-seventies burnt orange colour inside. Unoccupied for sometime in between times, its last use had been as an Off Licence and at one time it was part of the Arthur Cooper chain - before that however it had been a pub and a pub with a rather unusual name - the Which You Please.

Standing on the corner of Keyham Road and St. Levan Road, the photograph we see here shows us that even in the first decades of this century this was no ordinary pub. Situated across the road from the Avondale and opposite the dockyard gate, this was a pub and a general store all rolled into one. J.H. Ellis was here from around 1900 through almost to 1920 and, as it is his name above the door, the photograph is most likely to be of him and his family.

PLYMOUTH

P**U**BS

PAST & PRESENT

THE WOODSIDE

The large stone tablet above the Park Terrace sign tells us that "near this spot stood a gate" - the Gasking or Gascoyne Gate. The gate was one of the old town gates and was located at what was then the north eastern entrance to the town, indeed Gasking Street was once known as North Gate Street. In 1768 this gate was pulled down - for street widening. It should be remembered that before the construction of the Embankment in the early nineteenth century the principal eastern route out of the town was down over Lipson Hill and Lipson Road effectively starts here. Although Gasking Street itself existed in 1768 beyond it there was little else other than fields and trees and one of the first major housing developments beyond this point, after the gate came down, was the row of properties known as Woodside. Long since surrounded by other developments Woodside still stands today, as does the pub which since the early nineteenth century at least has echoed its name. But no longer. The Woodside, like the Nottingham was refurbished by the Firkin chain and has, sadly, become the Fool and Firkin while even more lamentably the Nottingham is now the Freebooter and Firkin.

PLYMOUTH PUBS PAST & PRESENT

WYNDHAM ARMS

Wyndham Square is one of the more impressive early nineteenth century developments surviving in Plymouth today. The architect John Foulston was responsible for some of the work here and the Wyndham Arms, on the corner of the Square and Stoke Road is clearly contemporary with it. Originally a beer house, the pub quite possibly dates from the early 1830s when, following the 1830 Beer Act, some 35,000 new public houses were opened in England and Wales in just three years. The act permitted any ratepayer to be granted a licence for £2 to brew and sell beer on their premises.

Situated across from the wall of the Royal Naval Hospital, it is thought that under one of the great stone slabs in the cellar there is a tunnel that runs under the road, under the wall and comes out somewhere in the Hospital.

PLYMOUTH
PUBS
PAST & PRESENT

INDEX